sweet treats

sweet treats is proudly
presented by frankie magazine

sweet treats and frankie
magazine is proudly published
by morrison media

editor louise bannister
creative director/designer lara burke
photographer cath conroy
chef and food stylist mark core
digital operator alan jensen
publisher di josipovic
production manager john harland
circulation manager hayleigh baker

**want to order copies for your
shop?** contact hayleigh baker
hayleigh@morrisonmedia.com.au
+61 7 5576 1388

**want to order more copies for
yourself?** contact +61 7 5576 1388
or subs@morrisonmedia.com.au or
order online www.frankie.com.au

ISBN 978-0-9805354-4-0

www.morrisonmedia.com.au

www.frankie.com.au

this book belongs to...

_____

the
team

LARA BURKE
CREATIVE DIRECTOR & STYLIST

When Lara isn't scouring antique shops with her (very cute) son Milo, she's helming the design chair at frankie magazine and nutting out new pretty projects. This book taught her "chocolate is very messy" and that coconut ice is still her all-time favourite sweet.

LOUISE BANNISTER
EDITOR

Louise can usually be found pottering about her herb garden or brainstorming ideas for frankie magazine special projects. She considers herself an expert on marshmallows and so thought it only fair to be on hand to taste test (and sometimes fix Mark's recipe spelling errors).

MARK CORE
FOOD STYLIST & CHEF

Munching on Florentines, and hanging out with his kids are high on Mark's favourite things to do list. Although an expert on all things sweet and delicious, Mark claims he learnt something new in the making of this book; "The older I get the harder it is removing toffee from my teeth".

CATH CONROY
PHOTOGRAPHER

These days super snapper Cath splits her time between Amsterdam where she shoots fashion and Australia (where she enjoys mint patties). She loves finding her way around a new city and can't wait to finally visit New York in the summer.

ALAN JENSEN
DIGITAL OPERATOR

When Al isn't working on his beard or learning Dutch, he's dreaming of peanut brittle and skiing in Paris. A master of making photographs look their best, working on this book taught him the important lesson that beer and sweets don't mix.

this little book is
dedicated to
anyone who ever
lined up at the
tuckshop or
rushed straight
to the school
fete cake stall x

When you taste these recipes from long ago it's like savouring a distant memory, except the memories taste sweet and buttery. These treats remind us of people and places and a time when generous lashings of real sugar and butter were proudly packed into every yummy indulgence. They celebrate the time before preservatives ruled and calories were counted. And like all memories they come in different shapes and textures. Some are sharp and brittle, some are soft and squishy and others are sweet and gooey.

contents

here are answers to some questions you may have...

What equipment will make things easier for me?

If you don't have the following you could always improvise, but it'll make things easier if you can get your hands on these items.

- Scales
- Candy thermometer
- Wooden spoon
- Heatproof bowl
- Measuring cups
- Measuring spoons
- Heavy-based saucepan
- Greaseproof paper
- Baking tins
- Hand-held electric or bench-top mixer

Do I need electric mixer/beaters or can I beat everything with a spoon?

Depending on your mixing skills, you could make everything with a wooden spoon. But for minties and nougat, it's best to use an electric beater.

Do I need a candy thermometer? Where do I get one from?

It would be best if you had one. It'll make things a little easier and you won't have to take any extra steps to ensure you're at the right temperature. You can buy candy thermometers from most kitchen stores. You can pay anywhere from $12.

There are more expensive ones on the market, but you don't need to spend a lot to make the recipes in this book. To test your thermometer, put it in boiling water and it should read 100°C (at sea level). If it reads higher or lower, then adjust accordingly when you use it.

What does soft ball, hard ball and all those stages mean?

Good question. They're useful if you decide not to buy a candy thermometer. Have a look at the table on page 13 to see what each stage means.

How do I prevent burning myself when dealing with sticky, hot toffee?

Food-handling gloves can help, but the best thing to do is wait until the toffee is cool enough to handle. Also wear shoes, because when toffee falls on naked tootsies it really hurts.

How do I clean my pans after dealing with toffee and other sticky stuff?

Fill your pans with water and place back on the heat. Bring to a slow boil until toffee has liquefied and then pour out your water and wipe clean. If your sugar thermometer is covered in toffee, just clip it to the side of the pan you're cleaning. Don't submerge it though, as it'll ruin it.

. . . .

Is making candy difficult?

We've given a difficulty rating for each recipe. Zero being super simple, six being the most difficult. None of the recipes are very difficult, some just require more time and effort which can make them seem a little complicated. Also, because you might not have made this type of food before, don't be disappointed if things don't turn out perfect the first time. To prevent any confusion, it's important to read through the entire recipe before starting, just so you know what you're in for.

. . . .

What should I know before I start cooking?

It helps to use a wet spoon to get glucose out of a container. For most recipes it's important to brush down the sides of your pan with a wet pastry brush to prevent sugar from crystalising, however, read each recipe to make sure this is required (ie Joyce's Sugar Peanuts doesn't use this technique because you want the sugar to crystalise). Humid or rainy days affect sugar. It's best to cook a lot of this stuff on a dry day. For this book we lightly sprayed our greaseproof paper with canola oil, just to make sure our sweets slipped out when we wanted them to. Patience and a clean workspace are the two most

important things when making this kind of food. If something doesn't work, take a deep breath and try again. Let everything reach the right temperatures before beginning the next step. When whisking egg whites, it's essential to have a clean, dry bowl. We like to squeeze a little fresh lemon juice in the bowl to rid of any impurities. Make sure you wipe out the juice with a paper towel before starting.

. . . .

Can I melt chocolate in the microwave or do I have to melt it in a pan like instructed?

Yes, you can melt chocolate in the microwave, but make sure it's in a heatproof bowl and that you heat it in short bursts (10-15-second intervals).

. . . .

What if I don't have the exact tin that you ask or wire cooling racks, etc?

Just make do with similar-size tins or plastic containers and just use common sense if you don't have all the right stuff. For example, if you need a wire rack to cool something, just try to elevate your tin. You could prop your tin on four cans, just high enough to get air underneath it.

What if a recipe doesn't work?

All the recipes in this book have been well tested so we're confident they'll work for you. But, if you're having trouble with something, re-read the recipe, make sure you've included all the ingredients and followed the correct procedures.

. . . .

Why do you use couverture chocolate and where can I find it?

Couverture chocolate is a higher-quality chocolate that contains extra cocoa butter. The end result is a creamier, yummier, smoother-tasting chocolate. You can find couverture chocolate in specialty kitchen stores and delis. But don't despair if you can't find any or you find it too expensive, because everything will still taste great with a high-quality chocolate. Just use a chocolate that you like eating, there's no need to use actual cooking chocolate.

. . . .

I keep burning myself! What's the deal?

Try to slow things up and don't put your hand in the hot stuff too soon. Only handle mixtures when they're cool enough. If you do burn yourself, run your burnt bit under cold water – don't use ice.

stages
of
heating
sugar

THREAD STAGE
110°C - 112°C

Put a small amount of the syrup on to a spoon, and drop it into a glass of cold water. If it's like a spider web, it's ready.

SOFT-BALL STAGE
112°C - 115°C

Drop a small amount of syrup into a glass of cold water and it should form a soft, flexible ball.

FIRM-BALL STAGE
118°C - 120°C

When dropped in a glass of cold water a firm ball will form. You won't be able to flatten this unless you squeeze it.

HARD-BALL STAGE
121°C - 130°C

When dropped into a cup of chilled water, syrup will form into a hard ball, that will still change shape if you squash it.

SOFT-CRACK STAGE
132°C - 143°C

When dropped into ice water syrup will separate into hard but flexible threads. They will bend slightly before breaking.

HARD-CRACK STAGE
146°C - 154°C

If you drop syrup into chilled water it will separate into hard, brittle threads that break when bent.

best-ever peanut brittle

Line workbench with greaseproof paper (approx 50cm long).

Over low heat in a heavy-bottomed, medium saucepan, cook the sugar, glucose syrup and water until sugar is dissolved. Stir occasionally until temperature reaches 129°C (hard-ball stage).

Add nuts and butter and cook until temperature reaches 143°C (soft-crack stage). Make sure you stir constantly. (Brush sugar crystals from the sides of pan using wet pastry brush to prevent sugar from crystallising.) Take off the heat and stir in vanilla extract and bicarbonate soda quickly.

Pour mixture out on to greaseproof paper and spread out with an oiled spatula nice and thin. When the brittle begins to set, pull and stretch the brittle as much as possible. Let it cool before breaking into pieces.

Store the brittle in an airtight container at room temperature.

Makes a 50cm tray.

INGREDIENTS

· · · · · · · · · · · · · · ·

1 cup salted peanuts

1/2 cup glucose syrup

2 tablespoons water

1 1/2 tablespoons unsalted butter

1/2 teaspoon vanilla extract

1 teaspoon bicarbonate soda

1 cup caster sugar

LEVEL OF DIFFICULTY

sticky apples

Line a baking tray with baking paper. Spear a stick into each apple about 2/3 of the way in. Check to see they go in straight.

Over low heat, cook sugar and water in a medium saucepan. Stir until sugar has dissolved and then bring to boil without stirring. (To prevent sugar crystallising, brush down sides of pan with a wet pastry brush.)

Add food colouring and cream of tartar and give it a stir.

Reduce heat to low and simmer mixture for 20 minutes or until it reaches 150°C (hard-crack stage). Take off the heat immediately.

When toffee ceases bubbling, dip each apple into the toffee. You can coat an apple evenly by tipping the pan on an angle. Make sure you get lots of sticky stuff around the top of the stick, so it doesn't fall out when you hold it.

Put all sticky apples on to baking trays and set at room temperature. They'll set in about 30 minutes.

Best eaten straight away, but you can store them in an airtight container in a cool, dry place for up to 24 hours.

Makes 8 apples.

INGREDIENTS

8 small red apples, washed and air dried

2 cups caster sugar

1/2 cup water

1/4 teaspoon cream of tartar

1 teaspoon red food colouring

8 wooden sticks

LEVEL OF DIFFICULTY

candy hearts

Line a couple of trays with baking paper. In a small saucepan over low heat, heat the glucose syrup, water and gelatine only until the gelatine has dissolved. Take pan off the heat and stir mixture.

Grab a large bowl and electric hand mixer. Transfer the mixture into the bowl along with 1/3 of the icing sugar. Mix on low speed until everything is combined.

Add another 1/3 of the icing sugar and continue mixing on low speed until the mixture is smooth. Add the remaining sugar until mixed in. Keep going until your mixture transforms into firm dough.

Now throw some sugar on your workbench and prepare to start kneading your dough. Transfer the dough to the workbench and begin to knead. Use as much icing sugar as you need to dust your dough as it will make it easier to work with. When the dough turns shiny, stop kneading.

Cut the dough into as many pieces as you'd like to colour. Take a piece of dough and use the bench to flatten it. Drop the red food colouring and your choice of flavouring on to your flat piece and combine your colour and flavour by kneading. Do the same for all your pieces. Wrap each coloured piece in cling film to stop the mixture from drying. Using a rolling pin, roll out the dough on to a piece of greaseproof paper and prepare to cut into shapes.

Once you've cut your chosen shapes, pop them on your trays and allow to air dry for at least a full day.

When they're completely dry, use your stamp set or icing pen to write sweet notes. (If you're using a stamping set, you can start stamping straight away, while mixture is still soft. But if you're using a pen, best to wait until they're completely dry.)

Store between baking sheets in an airtight container.

Makes approximately 30-40 small hearts.

INGREDIENTS

1 teaspoon unflavoured gelatine

1/4 cup water

1 teaspoon glucose syrup

500g icing sugar, plus additional for rolling and dusting

Flavouring extract of your choice (mint, orange, etc)

Red food colouring

Heart-shaped cutter (or whatever shapes you like)

Stamping set or icing pen (we used a stamping set)

LEVEL OF DIFFICULTY

fruity jelly chews

Grease a 6-inch cake tin. Put gelatine and cold water in a small bowl. Leave it to sit for 5-10 minutes.

Over low heat combine hot water and sugar in a heavy-bottomed, small saucepan. Without boiling, stir in the sugar until dissolved.

Take sugar mixture off the heat and pour in the gelatine mixture and food colouring, whisk until well combined. Pop back on medium heat and boil mixture gradually for 15 minutes, whisking occasionally (watch out with this step as it's super easy to burn the mixture). Take off the heat and add orange and lemon juice.

Pour mixture into your cake tin and refrigerate until firm (at least 3 hours). Once set transfer jelly mixture on to lightly greased paper laid over a chopping board.

Prepare a second sheet of baking paper and cover with caster sugar. Cut jelly into cubes and coat in sugar.

Store at room temperature in an airtight container.

Makes approximately 35 jellies.

INGREDIENTS

1/3 cup orange juice

1 tablespoon lemon juice

3 tablespoons unflavoured powdered gelatine

1/2 cup cold water

1/2 cup hot water

2 cups caster sugar

1/4 cup glucose syrup

Few drops food colouring (whatever you fancy)

LEVEL OF DIFFICULTY

cream caramels

Line an 8-inch tin with greaseproof paper. Pop the stove on medium heat and grab a medium-sized, heavy bottomed saucepan.

Pour in caster sugar, glucose syrup, milk, cream and butter and stir until sugar has dissolved. Keep stirring until the mixture reaches 120°C (firm-ball stage).

Pull the pan off the heat and stir in vanilla extract.

Pour mixture into tin and let cool. Best to let it set overnight.

Turn out of tin on to a chopping board and with a sharp knife cut into squares. Store in an airtight container between sheets of greaseproof paper.

Makes approximately 30 squares.

INGREDIENTS

1 1/2 cups caster sugar

1/2 cup glucose syrup

1/2 cup milk

285ml thickened cream

1/2 cup unsalted butter

1/4 teaspoon vanilla extract

LEVEL OF DIFFICULTY

marshmallow cones

Place ice-cream cones on a tray. Pour sugar, gelatine and water into a medium saucepan and stir until dissolved.

Pop on low heat and boil for 10 minutes without stirring. Take pan off heat and let it settle for 10 minutes.

Add vanilla extract and beat the mixture until it becomes creamy and delicious (about 10 minutes).

Start spooning the marshmallow mixture into each cone, making sure the cone is filled from the bottom. Using your spoon, create an ice-cream cone shape on top.

Sprinkle with 100s and 1000s and aside until set for about an hour. Once set, store in an airtight container at room temperature.

Makes 12.

INGREDIENTS

1 cup caster sugar

1 tablespoon gelatine

2/3 cup water

1/2 teaspoon vanilla extract

100s and 1000s

12 flat-bottomed ice-cream cones

LEVEL OF DIFFICULTY

coconut ice

Lightly grease an 8-inch square tin. Put the Copha in a small saucepan and melt over low heat.

In a large bowl lightly beat egg whites. Add coconut, Copha, icing-sugar mixture and vanilla extract. Mix together until well combined.

Split the mixture into two equal parts and press one half of the mixture into your pan. Stir and mix food colouring into the other half (hands are good for this) until it turns pink.

Press pink mixture on top of the plain mixture. Cover in cling film and pop in the fridge for 45 minutes or until it sets.

When set, turn on to chopping board and cut into whatever shape you like.

Makes 10-12.

INGREDIENTS

. . . .

250g icing-sugar mixture

60g Copha

125g desiccated coconut

1 egg white

1-2 drops vanilla extract

Few drops red/pink food colouring

LEVEL OF DIFFICULTY

joyce's sugar peanuts

Line a baking tray with greaseproof paper. Mix ingredients in a large bowl until peanuts are well coated.

Pop a frypan over medium heat and place in all ingredients. Jiggle the pan occasionally to make sure all the nuts are coated and sugar doesn't burn. This will take about 20-25 minutes.

When liquid has evaporated and peanuts have a coating of crystallised sugar, take off heat and pour on to baking tray.

Cool at room temperature for about 30 minutes and place in an airtight container.

Makes enough for a medium-sized jar.

INGREDIENTS

· · · · · · · · · · · · · · · · · ·

250g raw peanuts (with red skin on)

1 cup caster sugar

1/2 cup water

2 teaspoons red food colouring

LEVEL OF DIFFICULTY

mint-patty delights

Line one tray with greaseproof paper and prepare a workbench with a dusting of icing sugar.

Take a large bowl and pour in condensed milk, mint extract and food colouring. Mix until combined.

Add icing sugar and beat with an electric mixer on low speed until mixture becomes smooth. Pour mixture on to your sugary workbench.

Knead the mixture gently until you've got a nice, smooth ball. Pull off pieces of the mixture and shape into balls. Flatten each ball into discs on the tray. Pop in the fridge and let them set for 1 1/2 hours.

Meanwhile boil some water in a saucepan and fit with a heatproof bowl (make sure the water doesn't touch the bowl). Turn the hotplate down low and melt the chocolate in the bowl.

Brush one side of the patty with melted chocolate and transfer to a tray lined with greaseproof paper. Set in fridge.

Store in an airtight container in the fridge.

Make approximately 24 patties.

INGREDIENTS

. . . .

1/2 can sweetened condensed milk

1/2 tablespoon mint extract

4 cups icing sugar

100g dark couverture chocolate (or any good-quality cooking chocolate)

Green food colouring

LEVEL OF DIFFICULTY

apricot balls

Chop apricots into small pieces and place in a large bowl. Add the honey and mix well until sticky and combined (clean hands are good for this). Place coconut in a separate bowl.

Spoon out tablespoons of apricot mixture and roll into balls, then roll the balls in the shredded coconut.

Place balls in an airtight container between layers of baking paper.

INGREDIENTS

200g dried apricots

1 1/2 tablespoons honey

1 cup shredded coconut

LEVEL OF DIFFICULTY

caramel fudge

Line an 8-inch square baking tin with greaseproof paper.

In a medium-size saucepan, over medium heat bring one cup of sugar and water to a light caramel colour.

Slowly pour in cream and 2 cups of sugar. Now add glucose syrup, butter and salt.

Cook until mixture reaches 115°C on the candy thermometer (soft-ball stage).

Take mixture off the heat and allow to cool for about 5–10 minutes.

Transfer to a bowl and beat with a wooden spoon until mixture thickens and loses its shine (about 10-15 minutes).

Turn the fudge into prepared tin and set at room temperature until hard (this will take at least an hour).

Turn out on to chopping board and cut into squares. Store in an airtight container between sheets of greaseproof paper.

Makes approximately 24 pieces.

INGREDIENTS

· · · · · · · · · · · · · · · ·

3 cups caster sugar

1 tablespoon water

1 cup thickened cream

2 tablespoons glucose syrup

1/4 cup unsalted butter

Pinch of salt

LEVEL OF DIFFICULTY

choccie fudge

Line an 8-inch square tin with greaseproof paper.

Mix all ingredients except vanilla extract in a saucepan and heat slowly on low heat, stirring until the sugar is dissolved and chocolate has melted. (To prevent sugar crystallising, brush down sides of pan with a wet pastry brush.)

Increase heat to medium and slowly bring to the boil stirring occasionally until temperature reaches 112 (soft-ball stage).

Remove from heat and mix in vanilla extract. Cooling will take about 5-10 minutes.

Beat with a wooden spoon until mixture thickens and loses its gloss (about 10-15 minutes). Pour into tin. Allow to cool and set at room temperature for at least an hour. Once set turn fudge on to chopping board and cut into squares. Store in an airtight container between sheets of greaseproof paper.

Makes approximately 24 pieces.

INGREDIENTS

· · · · · · · · · · · · · ·

2 cups of caster sugar

100g dark chocolate, chopped

2/3 cup of milk

2 tablespoons glucose syrup

2 tablespoons unsalted butter

Pinch of salt

1 teaspoon vanilla extract

coffee fudge

Line an 8-inch square baking tin with greaseproof paper.

Over low heat, place coffee, sugar, thickened cream, salt, cream of tartar and butter in a large, heavy-bottomed saucepan. Stir until sugar has dissolved. Over medium heat, bring the mixture to a boil. To prevent sugar crystallising, brush down sides of pan with a wet pastry brush.

Continue to cook mixture, without stirring until temperature reaches 112°C (soft-ball stage). This will take about 12-15 minutes.

Remove from heat and let mixture cool for about 10-15 minutes.

Transfer to a bowl and beat with a wooden spoon until mixture thickens and loses its gloss (about 10-15 minutes).

Pour the fudge into baking tin and allow to cool for at least an hour. Turn out on to chopping board and cut into squares. Store in an airtight container between sheets of greaseproof paper.

Makes approximately 24 pieces.

INGREDIENTS

1 1/2 tablespoons unsalted butter

3 tablespoons instant coffee powder dissolved in 1 cup of water

3 cups caster sugar

1 1/2 cups thickened cream

Pinch of salt

1/2 tsp cream of tartar

1/2 teaspoon vanilla extract

LEVEL OF DIFFICULTY

florentines

Preheat your oven to 170°C and lightly grease a couple of muffin baking trays. Pop your stove on a medium heat and grab a medium-sized saucepan.

Pour in the butter, honey, sugar and cream and stir constantly until your mixture reaches 120°C (firm-ball stage) on the candy thermometer. Throw in the flour and almonds and mix quickly until completely blended. Turn off the heat and remove pan.

Spoon the mixture into your muffin trays and flatten down to create a disc-type shape.

Bake in the oven for about 10-12 minutes until golden brown.

Meanwhile, boil a little water in a saucepan and attach a heatproof bowl firmly on top (the water should not touch the bowl). Over low heat melt the chocolate and set aside.

Cool the muffin trays for about 3-5 minutes and then turn them on to a wire rack.

Dip one half of the Florentine into the melted chocolate and set on to a baking tray lined with greaseproof paper. Pop in the fridge for about 15 minutes until chocolate sets. Store between sheets of baking paper in an airtight container in the fridge.

Makes about 12.

INGREDIENTS

5 tablespoons unsalted butter

1/3 cup caster sugar

1 tablespoon honey

1 1/2 tablespoon thickened cream

50g couverture chocolate

1 cup flaked almonds

1 tablespoon plain flour

LEVEL OF DIFFICULTY

pistachio nougat

Line an 8-inch tin with greaseproof paper.

Pop your stove on low heat. Pour sugar, water and glucose syrup into a medium-sized saucepan and cook, stirring until the sugar has dissolved.

Take off the heat, and to prevent sugar crystallising brush down sides of pan with a wet pastry brush.

Turn up the heat to moderate and continue cooking for about 2 minutes, until mixture boils. Keep brushing down sides of pan to remove any sugar.

Stop stirring, turn the heat down low and pop in the candy thermometer. Keep cooking until the thermometer reaches 143°C (soft-crack stage). Meanwhile, in a separate heatproof bowl beat your egg white until stiff peaks form.

Once your mixture has reached 143°C, pour the hot syrup slowly over the beaten egg white. Make sure you're beating constantly until the mixture becomes thick.

Beat in the pistachios and vanilla extract and then turn mixture into your greased tin. Let stand at room temperature for at least 24 hours.

Turn out nougat on to chopping board and with a super-sharp knife cut into squares. Store between sheets of baking paper in an airtight container.

Makes 18-24.

INGREDIENTS

. . . .

1 egg white, at room temperature

1 1/2 cups caster sugar

1/2 cup glucose syrup

1/2 cup water

1 teaspoon vanilla extract

1 cup shelled pistachios

LEVEL OF DIFFICULTY

sugary sherbet

Dry down your workbench before you begin. If anything's wet, the sherbet won't come together correctly.

Sift the icing sugar into a plastic container. Pour in citric acid and bicarbonate soda and mix well.

Grind the contents into a fine powder with a knife or the back of a spoon. Add in a dried food colouring of your choice.

Store your sherbet in an airtight container.

· · · · · · · · · · · · · · · · · ·

3 tablespoons citric acid

1 tablespoon bicarbonate soda

10 tablespoons icing sugar

Powdered food colouring

musk sticks

Line a couple of trays with baking paper. In a small saucepan over low heat, heat the glucose syrup, water and gelatine only until the gelatine has dissolved.

Take pan off the heat and stir mixture.

Grab a large bowl and electric hand mixer. Transfer the mixture into the bowl along with 1/3 of the icing sugar. Mix on low speed until everything is combined.

Add another 1/3 of the icing sugar and continue mixing on low speed until the mixture is smooth. Add the remaining sugar, colour and flavouring and beat until combined.

Transfer to a piping bag with a 1cm star nozzle and start to pipe around 4-inch sticks on to your baking trays. Allow your musk sticks to air dry for 6 to 8 hours.

Store in airtight container at room temperature.

Make approximately 20.

INGREDIENTS

. . . .

1 teaspoon unflavoured gelatine

1/3 cup water

1 teaspoon glucose syrup

500g icing sugar, plus additional for rolling and dusting

1-2 teaspoons musk flavouring (or a flavouring of your choice)

Few drops pink food colouring

Piping bag with 1cm star nozzle (You can buy these from the supermarket)

LEVEL OF DIFFICULTY

coconutty shuku shuku

Turn the oven up to 175°C and line a baking tray with greaseproof paper.

In a large bowl, mix together sugar, coconut and egg yolks until the mixture forms a firm, dough-like consistency.

Pick up a little mixture with a teaspoon and begin to form marble-size balls. Roll them through flour and drop on to your baking tray.

Put tray in the oven and bake for 15-20 minutes until golden.

Cool the balls on a wire rack, roll in icing sugar and keep in airtight container.

Makes approximately 30 balls.

· · · · · · · · · · · · · · · · ·

80g desiccated coconut

60g caster sugar

3 egg yolks

60g self-raising flour
(for rolling)

1/4 cup icing sugar
(for dusting, after cooled)

choc macadamias

Preheat oven to 170°C. Line a baking tray with greaseproof paper. Place macadamias on tray and roast for 6-8 minutes or until golden brown. Halve macadamias and set aside.

Boil a little water in a saucepan and attach a heatproof bowl firmly on top (the water should not touch the bowl). Over low heat melt chocolate.

Lightly grease chocolate mould and place halved macadamias in each mould. Pour chocolate slowly over macadamias. Pour only enough to fill each mould.

Refrigerate for 40 minutes or until set. Store in airtight container in fridge.

Makes 18-20 depending on your mould.

INGREDIENTS

. . . .

200g good-quality milk, dark or coloured chocolate

200g roasted macadamias, halved

A chocolate mould of your choice

LEVEL OF DIFFICULTY

caramel popcorn balls

Line a baking tray with baking paper. Heat oil in a large, heavy-bottomed saucepan over medium heat.

Add the corn kernels and give it a stir. Hold the lid of the saucepan tightly and shake occasionally. Cook until all the popcorn stops popping. Pour the cooked popcorn in a large bowl and put to the side.

In a small, heavy-bottomed saucepan mix sugar, butter, honey and cream and stir over medium heat until sugar has dissolved. Don't let the mixture boil. To prevent sugar crystallising, brush down sides of pan with a wet pastry brush.

Now, bring to the boil without stirring for 7-10 minutes.

Pour the gooey syrup over the popcorn and coat thoroughly. When mixture has cooled enough to handle, oil up your hands and shape the popcorn into balls.

Place on baking tray and allow to set for 30 minutes.

Store in airtight container in a cool, dry place.

Makes approximately 24 balls.

INGREDIENTS

. . . .

2 tablespoons vegetable oil

1/2 cup popping corn kernels

1 cup caster sugar

120g unsalted butter

2 tablespoons honey

1/2 cup thickened cream

LEVEL OF DIFFICULTY

sweet honeycomb

Stretch out 60cm of baking paper and line your workbench. In a heavy-bottomed, large saucepan, over medium heat, mix together caster sugar, glucose, honey and water and bring to the boil. You want the mixture to become a caramel colour, so keep cooking until it looks golden.

Take mixture off the heat. Get yourself a whisk, pour in the bicarbonate of soda and beat quickly. The mixture will foam up and double in size.

Turn the mixture out evenly on to your baking paper and wait for it to set. This will take about 45 minutes.

Once cool and set, split honeycomb into pieces and store in airtight container. Moisture will make your honeycomb soft, so it's important to keep it dry.

Makes large slab.

INGREDIENTS

· · · · · · · · · · · · · · ·

330g caster sugar

15g bicarbonate soda

130ml liquid glucose

60g honey

1/4 cup water

LEVEL OF DIFFICULTY

lollipops

Pop the stove on low to medium heat. Add sugar, water, cream of tartar and glucose syrup to a large, heavy-bottomed saucepan and mix until sugar dissolved. Continue cooking (but don't stir) until the mixture reaches 130°C (hard-ball stage).

Turn off the heat and put the pan aside. Now drop in your flavour.

Split the mixture into two and pour one half into a second saucepan. Mix the chosen food colouring into your two parts. (A mixture without food colouring turns white, so no need to mix any food colouring if you want white as one of your colours.)

Lay out some greaseproof paper on a workbench. While the mixture is cooling move the mixture back and forth with a chopstick or knife. Don't stir; just gently pull up and down.

Allow the candy to cool so you can pick it up without it burning your hands. (This takes about 20 minutes – half an hour. Best to check it CAREFULLY every 10 minutes.) Grease up your hands with oil and both you and your helper pull out a smallish piece of each mixture.

Start pulling and folding the piece with your hands until the candy starts looking shiny. Now, roll your piece into a thick rope. This bit can be tricky if your workbench is slippery. Try and work where there is grip or alternate between rolling the mixture between your hands and on the bench.

Intertwine the two candy ropes and roll them together into one rope. Pop the rope on the bench. Start curling the rope around itself so it makes a circle. Keep going until you have the size you want.

Pop the lollipop on to the baking paper and press a chopstick into it. Let the lollipop set for a couple of hours. Wrap in cling film if you're not eating it straight away.

Makes 2-4 depending on size.

INGREDIENTS

. . . .

1 cup caster sugar

1/2 teaspoon flavouring extract (whatever you fancy)

Good pinch cream of tartar

1/4 cup glucose syrup

1/4 cup water

1/4 teaspoon food colouring (per colour)

Oil for hands

Chopsticks

A helper to speed things along

WARNING: Be very careful making lollipops as the mixture can burn you easily.

LEVEL OF DIFFICULTY

sesame-seed brittle

Pop some greaseproof paper in a shallow baking tin and set aside. Take a heavy-bottomed medium saucepan and add sugar and water. Bring to the boil over low to medium heat and stir until all the sugar has dissolved

Spoon in the glucose syrup and keep cooking, but stop stirring, until your mixture reaches 115°C (soft-ball stage).

Throw in the sesame seeds and over moderate heat stir constantly. Cook until mixture turns golden caramel in colour and temperature reaches 143°C (soft-crack stage).

Take mixture off the heat, add butter and baking soda and mix until combined. Pour mixture on to prepared tray and allow to set at room temperature for 45 minutes. Break into pieces and store in an airtight container at room temperature.

Makes one 12-inch-tray.

1 cup sesame seeds

1/2 cup caster sugar

1/2 cup glucose syrup

1/4 cup water

1 tablespoon unsalted butter

1/2 teaspoon baking soda

LEVEL OF DIFFICULTY

choc truffles

Break or chop chocolate into small pieces and place in heatproof bowl. Add cream to a saucepan and bring to a simmer over medium heat.

Pour the hot cream and dark rum over the chocolate and stir until combined and shiny.

Pop the mixture in the fridge for 1 1/2 hours until firm.

To make truffles, roll the cool mixture into small balls. Dust with sifted cocoa powder. Store in the fridge in an airtight container between sheets of baking paper.

Makes approximately 40 marble-size balls.

INGREDIENTS

300g dark couverture chocolate

200mls thickened cream

15mls dark rum

Cocoa powder for dusting

vanilla truffles

Line two baking trays with greaseproof paper. Pour 250g white chocolate into a heatproof bowl.

In a small saucepan over low heat bring cream and vanilla pod seeds to a simmering point. To extract vanilla pod seeds, just scrape out with a knife. Be careful mixture doesn't boil.

Pour hot cream mixture over chocolate and stir until combined. Place mixture in fridge for about 1 1/2 hours until it sets.

Roll small teaspoon-size balls of the mixture and place them on one of the baking trays. Refrigerate for about 45 minutes or until set.

Meanwhile, boil a little water in a saucepan and attach a heatproof bowl firmly on top (the water should not touch the bowl). Over low heat melt the remaining 120g milk chocolate in the heatproof bowl.

Using a spoon to help, dip balls into melted chocolate. Shake off excess chocolate and place on second tray. Return to fridge for about 45 minutes until outer chocolate is set.

Store in the fridge in an airtight container between sheets of baking paper.

Makes approximately 40 marble size balls.

. . . .

250g white couverture chocolate

1/2 cup thickened cream

1 vanilla bean, spilt lengthways

120 g white couverture chocolate, extra

LEVEL OF DIFFICULTY

ginger truffles

Line two baking trays with greaseproof paper. Pour 225g milk chocolate and finely diced ginger into a heatproof bowl.

In a small saucepan over low heat bring cream to a simmering point. Be careful it doesn't boil.

Pour hot cream mixture over chocolate and stir until combined. Place mixture in fridge for about 1 1/2 hours until it sets.

Roll small teaspoon-size balls of the mixture and place them on one of the baking trays. Refrigerate for about 45 minutes or until set.

Meanwhile, boil a little water in a saucepan and attach a heatproof bowl firmly on top (the water should not touch the bowl). Over low heat melt the remaining 120g milk chocolate in the heatproof bowl.

Using a spoon, dip balls into melted chocolate. Shake off excess chocolate and place on second tray. Garnish with slice of ginger and return to fridge for about 45 minutes until outer chocolate is set.

Store in the fridge in an airtight container between sheets of baking paper. If you find it difficult to dip the balls into chocolate, you could always roll the balls in cocoa powder, icing sugar or coconut, or whatever you fancy.

Makes approximately 40 marble-size balls.

INGREDIENTS

225g couverture milk chocolate

1/2 cup thickened cream

1/2 cup finely diced crystallised ginger

Extra ginger finely sliced for garnish

120g couverture milk chocolate, extra

LEVEL OF DIFFICULTY

chocolate crackles

Pour Rice Bubbles, icing sugar and cocoa in a large bowl and mix well. Place the Copha in a small saucepan and over low heat melt slowly. Allow mixture to cool slightly and then add to Rice Bubbles mixture. Stir until well combined.

Spoon mixture into patty cases and refrigerate until set (about 30 minutes).

Makes approximately 20-24.

· · · · · · · · · · · · · · · ·

4 cups Kellogg's Rice Bubbles

1 cup icing sugar

200g Copha

4 tablespoons cocoa powder

24 patty cases

LEVEL OF DIFFICULTY

brown cow caramels

Line a plastic rectangle container with greaseproof paper.

Combine all ingredients in a medium, heavy-bottomed saucepan over low heat, stirring for about 5 minutes or until mixture comes to a boil. To prevent sugar crystallising, brush down sides of pan with a wet pastry brush.

Increase the heat to medium and cook mixture until temperature reaches 115 (soft-ball stage). This will take around 12-15 minutes. Keep stirring as the mixture sticks easily to the bottom of the pan.

Remove from heat and pour mixture into prepared plastic container. Cool completely at room temperature. Best to leave overnight.

Turn caramel on to a chopping board and cut into squares.

Makes approximately 24 squares.

· · · · · · · · · · · · · · · · ·

1/2 cup brown sugar

1/2 cup caster sugar

3/4 cup glucose syrup

3/4 cup condensed milk

1/4 cup unsalted butter

Pinch of salt

LEVEL OF DIFFICULTY

freckle hearts

Line a tray with baking paper. Lightly grease heart-shape cutters with a little butter or oil and place on baking paper.

Boil a little water in a saucepan and attach a heatproof bowl firmly on top (the water should not touch the bowl). Over low heat melt chocolate and Copha in the bowl.

Place about a tablespoon of chocolate mix into each cutter (may need more of less, depending on size of cutter). Cover with 100s and 1000s and refrigerate for 30 minutes or until set. Turn out of moulds and store in airtight container in the fridge.

Makes around 8-10.

INGREDIENTS

· · · · · · · · · · · · · · · · ·

250g good-quality milk
or dark chocolate

20g Copha, chopped

1/2 cup 100s and 1000s

LEVEL OF DIFFICULTY

sugared orange peel

Line a workbench with two separate sheets of baking paper.

Slice off ends of oranges and then cut into eighths leaving the flesh on. Put the orange slices in a heavy-bottomed, medium saucepan and pour in some water – just enough to cover the oranges. Bring to the boil over medium heat.

Once mixture is boiling, boil for a further 10 minutes. You want to repeat this process three times in total, so drain off the water and start again with fresh water, but now boil for 15 minutes each time.

After you have finished boiling for the third boil, transfer your orange slices to a strainer, and rinse under cold water. Now pull all excess pulp from the peel. Slice peel in half, lengthways.

In the saucepan, over low heat, mix 1 1/2 cups of caster sugar, orange peel, flavoured water and orange essence. Stir until sugar dissolves. Continue to cook over low heat for 1 1/4 hours, stirring every now and then. Take pan off the heat.

Dump remaining caster sugar on one piece of wax paper and coat the orange peel in the sugar. Drop peel on to the second sheet of baking paper and let it air dry for 35 minutes.

Refrigerate the peel in an airtight container.

Makes approximately 48 pieces.

INGREDIENTS

· · · · · · · · · · · · · · ·

3-4 large, thick-skinned oranges

3 cups caster sugar

1/2 cup of water with few drops of orange essence

1/4 teaspoon orange essence extra

LEVEL OF DIFFICULTY

coconut marshmallows

Line an 8-inch cake tin with greaseproof paper and lightly oil.
Place sugar, gelatine and water into a medium saucepan and stir
until dissolved. Pop on low heat and boil for 10 minutes without
stirring. Take pan off heat and let it settle for 10 minutes. Add your
choice of essence and beat with electric beater until it becomes
creamy and delicious (about 10 minutes). Transfer marshmallow
mixture to your tin and let it set for a couple of hours.

Meanwhile preheat oven to 160°C. Put coconut on a baking tray
lined with greaseproof paper and allow to roast for a couple of
minutes or until light golden brown. Keep an eye on your coconut
because it can burn quickly.

Once set, cut your marshmallows into whatever shape you like
and roll through toasted coconut.

Store in an airtight container at room temperature.

Makes approximately 24 squares.

INGREDIENTS

1 cup caster sugar

1 tablespoon gelatine

2/3 cup water

1/2 teaspoon coconut
or vanilla essence

1 cup desiccated coconut

LEVEL OF DIFFICULTY

old-school boiled lollies

Grease a 12-inch shallow slice tin. Now grease a baking sheet and place on the workbench.

Take a heavy-bottomed, large saucepan and add sugar, water and glucose syrup. Stir until sugar is dissolved. Stop stirring, lower the heat and cook gradually until temperature reaches 150°C (hard-crack stage).

Brush sugar crystals from the sides of pan using a wet pastry brush to prevent sugar from crystallising.

Take mixture off the heat and add strawberry extract and food colouring. Mix lightly. Transfer mixture into slice tin and wait for it to cool, only enough until you can pick it up with your hands.

Cut it with lightly greased large scissors into thin strips, and then quickly cut strips into pieces. Drop the snipped pieces on to your baking sheet. Lightly roll in icing sugar so they don't stick together and once completely cooled store in an airtight container.

Makes 50-60 pieces.

INGREDIENTS

1 cup water

3/4 cup glucose syrup

2 cups caster sugar

1/2 teaspoon strawberry extract

Few drops red food colouring

Icing sugar for dusting

LEVEL OF DIFFICULTY

cherry surprises

Line two baking trays with greaseproof paper and set aside.
In a large bowl mix coconut, cherries, food colouring and
condensed milk until well combined.

Roll into balls, place on one prepared tray and refrigerate for
about 30 minutes.

Boil a little water in a saucepan and attach a heatproof bowl firmly
on top (the water should not touch the bowl). Over low heat melt
the chocolate and Copha together in the heatproof bowl.

Using a spoon, dip balls into chocolate mixture and place on
your second prepared tray.

Let chocolate set in fridge for about 20 minutes.

Makes approximately 36.

INGREDIENTS

2 cups desiccated coconut

200g good-quality dark
chocolate

1/2 tin sweetened
condensed milk

200g glace cherries,
chopped

10g Copha

1 drop red food colouring

LEVEL OF DIFFICULTY

toffee patties

Lightly grease patty-cake papers and drop them in muffin trays.

Put all the ingredients into a heavy-bottomed, medium saucepan and stir over low heat until all the sugar has dissolved. Increase the heat to medium and boil without stirring until mixture reaches 150° (hard crack stage). To prevent sugar crystallising, brush down sides of pan with a wet pastry brush.

Take the mixture off the heat and pour into your patty-cake papers.

Sprinkle with 100s and 1000s and let set at room temperature until cool (this will take about 45 minutes). Pop in airtight container and store in a cool, dry place.

Makes 12-16 patty-cake cups.

INGREDIENTS

· · · · · · · · · · · · · · · · · ·

1 tablespoon unsalted butter

2 cups caster sugar

1 tablespoon white vinegar

3/4 cup water

100s and 1000s

12-16 patty cases

LEVEL OF DIFFICULTY

butterscotch sweets

Lightly grease a couple of chocolate moulds (enough to hold about 20 sweets).

In a large, heavy-bottomed saucepan over low heat, mix cream, sugar and water and keep stirring until sugar dissolves. Add cream of tartar.

Increase heat to medium and without stirring boil mixture until reaches 115°C (soft-ball stage). Add the chopped butter and boil until mixture reaches 135°C (soft-crack stage). Stir mixture occasionally.

Quickly drop teaspoon-size drops of butterscotch into your moulds. Set at room temperature in a dry, cool place for 45 minutes. Turn out of moulds and store in an airtight container.

Makes approximately 20.

INGREDIENTS

· · · · · · · · · · · · · · ·

2 cups caster sugar

2/3 cup thickened cream

2/3 cup of water

1/4 teaspoon cream of tartar

6 tbsp unsalted butter, cut into small pieces

LEVEL OF DIFFICULTY

honey joys

Lightly grease patty-cake cases. Preheat oven to 150.

Pour cornflakes into a bowl. Set aside.

In a small saucepan melt butter, sugar and honey over medium heat until frothy. Pour over cornflakes and mix well.

Spoon into patty-cake cases and pop on to a tray. Bake for 10 minutes. Allow to cool on cooling rack for 10 minutes.

Makes approximately 16-18.

INGREDIENTS

· · · · · · · · · · · · · · · · · ·

100g unsalted butter

1/3 cup caster sugar

2 tablespoons honey

4 cups cornflakes

LEVEL OF DIFFICULTY

mark's minties

Line an 8-inch by 8-inch square cake tin (or a tin close enough to this size) with greaseproof paper.

Heat medium, heavy-bottomed saucepan over low heat and pour in sugar, water and glucose syrup, Stir until sugar has dissolved. To prevent sugar crystallising, brush down sides of pan with a wet pastry brush.

Place egg white in a large heatproof bowl. Set aside.

Increase heat to medium and without stirring bring sugar mixture to a boil. When mixture reaches 125°C (hard-ball stage), use an electric beater to whip the egg whites until firm peaks form.

When sugar reaches 150°C (hard-crack stage), remove from heat With beater on medium speed, slowly pour hot syrup onto egg whites. Add mint flavour and colouring (optional) and beat for a further 2-3 minutes.

Quickly pour mixture into prepared tin and press down with a lightly oiled spoon. Mixture can also be poured into mini foil patty cases.

Allow to cool and harden at room temperature (around 2-3 hours).

Turn mintie slab on to chopping board and with a large, sharp knife cut into 3 cm squares. Lightly dust with icing sugar and place in an airtight container, layering minties between greaseproof paper. Store in a cool, dry place.

Makes approximately 20.

INGREDIENTS

1 1/4 cups caster sugar

1/4 cup water

250g glucose syrup

1 egg white (at room temperature)

Few drops green food colouring (optional)

3-4 teaspoon mint extract (depending on how you like your mintiness)

Icing sugar for dusting

LEVEL OF DIFFICULTY

roasted coconut roughs

Preheat oven to 170°C. On a baking tray spread out coconut evenly and place in preheated oven. Roast for about 4-5 minutes, until coconut is a light golden colour. Remove from oven and set aside to cool.

Line a flat baking tray with greaseproof paper and pace 6 lightly greased egg rings on the paper.

Boil a little water in a saucepan and attach a heatproof bowl firmly on top (The water should not touch the bowl). Over low heat melt chocolate and Copha in the bowl. Stir in coconut.

Place a heaped teaspoon of chocolate mixture into egg ring and smooth flat with back of spoon.

Refrigerate for 30 minutes or until set. Press out of egg rings and store in fridge in airtight container.

Makes 10-12.

INGREDIENTS

250g good-quality milk chocolate, chopped

10g Copha

1/2 cup desiccated coconut

turkish delight

Line an 8-inch cake tin with cling film. In a bowl mix together the glucose syrup and sugar. Set aside.

In a medium saucepan combine cornflour and water and whisk thoroughly. Place over low heat and simmer for 4-6 minutes, whisking continually (make sure there are no lumps). Add the glucose mixture to the cornflour mix. Keep stirring until the mixture reaches 102°C.

Take off the heat and mix in rosewater, citric acid and rose colouring (adding a drop at a time until the colour you want is reached).

Transfer mixture into the cake tin. Cover in a second piece of cling film and set for 12 hours.

Once set remove the cling film. In a small bowl mix extra icing sugar and extra cornflour together and sift evenly over jelly.

Turn the jelly out on to a chopping board and cut into whatever shapes you like. If you like, toss shapes in extra flour mix.

Store in an airtight container at room temperature.

Makes approximately 20.

INGREDIENTS
· · · · · · · · · · · · · · · · · · ·

60g cornflour

550mls water

120g glucose syrup

450g caster sugar

1/2 teaspoon rosewater

1/2 teaspoon citric acid

Red food colouring

3/4 cup icing sugar
(for dusting, extra)

1/4 cup cornflour
(for dusting, extra)

LEVEL OF DIFFICULTY

these pages
are for
you to paste
your own
sweet
recipes in x

notes

sweet thoughts.